Taking

Written by Greg Lang
Photography by Michael Curtain

My name is Emma.

I have a new camera.

I take pictures of my family with my new camera.

Dad was in the garden.

I went up and took his picture.

CLICK!

"That will be a good picture!"
I said.

Mom was in the bathroom.

I went up and took her picture.

CLICK!

"That will be a good picture!"
I said.

My brother was on the phone.

I went up and took his picture.

CLICK!

"That will be a good picture!"
I said.

My sister was in the yard.

I went up and took her picture.

CLICK!

"That will be a good picture!"
I said.

11

My grandpa was in the kitchen.

I went up and took his picture.

CLICK!

"That will be a good picture!"
I said.

13

This is my picture album.
Here are my pictures.

Smile!